SUPER AWESOME FACTS ABOUT EVERYTHING

RILEY WOLFE

Published by Astro Story Scope.

SCAN THIS
AND
GET OUR NEXT BOOK
FOR FREE!

CHAPTERS

WILDLIFE WONDERS

This acceleration is faster than most sports cars, including the Porsche 911 and the Lamborghini Huracan, making it one of the fastest accelerations in the animal kingdom.

The narwhal's tusk is actually a long, spiral tooth that can grow up to 10 feet (3 m) long, a unique physical feature among marine mammals.

A kangaroo loses its ability to jump if its tail is lifted off the ground, highlighting the importance of its tail for balance and locomotion.

The woodpecker's tongue wraps around its brain, providing protection while it pecks, a unique adaptation to its tree-boring lifestyle.

The basilisk lizard has the ability to run on water, a feat that's as impressive as it sounds and has earned it the nickname "Jesus Christ lizard".

Elephants are self-aware, able to recognize themselves in a mirror, a sign of high cognitive abilities.

Flamingos owe their pink hue to their diet, which includes shrimp and algae, a clear example of how diet can influence an animal's appearance.

A rhinoceros beetle can lift an astonishing 850 times its own weight, showcasing the incredible strength of this insect.

The pangolin is the only mammal covered in scales, giving it a unique, armored appearance that aids in its protection.

Chameleons change their color not to blend in with their surroundings, but to reflect their mood, a unique form of communication in the animal kingdom.

A shrimp's heart is located in its head, a unique anatomical feature not found in most animals.

These scales, made of keratin (the same material as human hair and nails), cover almost the entire body of the pangolin, providing an effective shield against predators

The mantis shrimp has an incredibly advanced vision, capable of seeing colors beyond human perception, a trait that aids in its predatory lifestyle.

Ants are incredibly strong for their size, able to carry up to 50 times their own body weight, a testament to their remarkable physical capabilities.

An octopus has three hearts and blue blood, making it one of the most unique creatures in the sea, both in terms of physiology and behavior.

A kangaroo is unable to walk backward, always progressing forward, a testament to its specialized locomotion.

The bumblebee bat, the world's smallest mammal, is so tiny it could fit on the tip of your finger, making it an incredibly unique species.

Native to the limestone caves in the forests of Thailand and Myanmar, this bat weighs around 2 grams (equivalent to a dime) and has a body length of just about 1.1 to 1.3 inches (2.8-3.3 cm).

The star-nosed mole is a speedy eater, consuming worms faster than the human eye can track, a necessary adaptation for its subterranean lifestyle.

Cows are known to form close friendships, often spending most of their time with a chosen companion, showing a level of social behavior that is quite complex.

The tongue of a blue whale is so large that 50 people could stand on it, highlighting the sheer size of the largest animal on Earth.

Seahorses are unique in the animal kingdom, as the males are the ones who give birth, a rare role reversal in terms of reproductive responsibilities.

This pendulous nose, hanging lower than the mouth, is believed to function as a resonating chamber, amplifying the monkey's vocalizations and thus helping males assert dominance and attract females

The blobfish, while appearing like a sad blob out of water, looks like a regular fish in its deep-sea home, demonstrating how pressure can affect an animal's appearance.

Bats hold the unique distinction of being the only mammals that can truly fly, a trait that sets them apart from all other mammals.

The tapeworm can grow up to an alarming 30 feet (9 m) long inside a host's body, a testament to the parasitic nature of these creatures.

A group of porcupines is aptly named a prickle, a fitting term for a group of these spiky rodents.

The horned lizard has a unique defense mechanism, shooting blood from its eyes to deter predators, a startling yet effective survival strategy.

The colugo, also known as the flying lemur, can glide through the air for over 200 feet (61 m), an impressive feat that aids in its arboreal lifestyle.

The dung beetle navigates using the stars, a remarkable feat for such a small creature, demonstrating a complexlevel of spatial awareness.

This stellar guidance helps them maintain a straight path as they roll balls of dung, often vastly heavier than themselves, across large distances for storage or nesting. This ability to employ celestial cues, despite their tiny brain, highlights the complexity of their spatial awareness, making dung beetles an intriguing subject for studies on animal navigation.

Sloths have a unique bathroom schedule, only pooping once a week, a behavior that helps them conserve energy.

Koalas are serious sleepers, clocking up to 22 hours a day in dreamland, a behavior that helps them conserve energy.

Giraffes require surprisingly little sleep, needing only 5 to 30 minutes per day, a sleep pattern that is quite unusual among mammals.

Penguins, while flightless, are excellent swimmers, gliding through the water with ease and speed that rivals many aquatic creatures.

Despite its cute appearance, the slow loris possesses a venomous bite, a rare trait among mammals that serves as a defense mechanism.

The male lyrebird is a master mimic, capable of replicating a wide range of sounds, from other bird calls to man-made noises.

Some frogs have the remarkable ability to freeze during the winter and thaw out in the spring, surviving in a state of suspended animation, a rare survival strategy in the animal kingdom.

Their eyes are roughly the size of a billiard ball and five times the size of the human eye! This combined with their height offers a broad visual field to detect predators like lions and cheetahs, key to their survival in their native African plains.

The sailfish, known as the fastest swimmer in the ocean, can reach speeds of up to 68 mph (109 kph), making it a formidable predator.

Squirrels are unable to burp or vomit, a unique trait among animals that is believed to be related to their diet and digestive system.

The mimic octopus is a master of disguise, able to change its shape and color to mimic other animals, a sophisticated form of camouflage.

The bombardier beetle has a unique defense mechanism, shooting boiling hot chemicals from its rear end, a startling yet effective way to deter predators.

Owls have an impressive range of neck motion, able to turn their heads up to 270 degrees, a feature that aids in their hunting prowess.

Male peacocks flaunt their bright and colorful feathers to attract a mate, a classic example of sexual selection in the animal kingdom.

Giraffes, despite their long necks, have the same number of neck bones as humans, a surprising fact given their distinct physical appearance.

Despite having a neck that can be up to eight feet long and weigh up to 600 pounds (272 kg), giraffes only have seven neck vertebrae - the same amount of neck bones as humans! However, unlike our vertebrae, theirs can grow to be up to 10 inches (25 cm) long.

Crocodiles are known for their longevity, with some living up to 100 years, making them one of the longest-living reptiles.

A group of jellyfish is interestingly called a smack, a term that reflects the collective behavior of these marine creatures.

A snail can sleep for up to three years, a testament to the slow-paced life of these creatures.

Dogs have an incredibly strong sense of smell, far surpassing that of humans, a trait that is often utilized in search and rescue operations.

A cat's purr has healing properties, aiding in the repair of bones and tissues, a fascinating example of the healing power of sound vibrations.

Some ants have a self-destructive defense mechanism, exploding to protect their colony, a dramatic example of altruism in the insect world.

A grizzly bear's bite is so powerful that it could crush a bowling ball, demonstrating the immense strength of this formidable creature.

Flamingos have a unique way of eating – they can only feed with their heads upside down!

Dogs indeed see colors, but not in the same way that we do. Their world is painted with shades similar to a color-blind human.

This is due to the number of "cones," cells in our eyes responsible for color detection. Humans have three types, allowing us to see a wide spectrum of colors, while dogs have two, enabling them to see mostly blue and yellow. So, a red ball on green grass to a dog would look like different shades of yellowish-gray. When choosing toys for dogs, blue or yellow ones might be more appealing to them.

Lions on average make just twenty kills in a year. Even more interestingly, it's the female lions, or lionesses, who do the majority of the hunting. They're responsible for a whopping ninety percent of these kills, demonstrating their crucial role in the survival of their prides.

If you put a goldfish in a room with no light, it actually changes color! Without sunlight, a goldfish can lose its vibrant hues and become quite pale.

Honey bees are ancient creatures that have been buzzing around for a long time! In fact, they've been on Earth for an astounding 30 million years. That's way before humans even existed!

SPACE FRONTIERS

Europa might hold an ocean under its icy surface that's possibly double the size of Earth's combined oceans. This moon is warmed by Jupiter's strong gravity, which could create conditions suitable for life, similar to Earth's deep-sea vents.

Uranus has a unique axial tilt that causes it to spin on its side. This unusual orientation is believed to be the result of a colossal collision in Uranus's past.

A day on Mercury, due to its slow rotation, lasts 1,408 Earth hours. This means that a single day-night cycle on Mercury is longer than its year, which is 88 Earth days.

A Martian day, also known as a sol, is 39 minutes and 35 seconds longer than a day on Earth. This slight difference in time is taken into account when planning the activities of Mars rovers.

The moon's temperature can fluctuate drastically, from extremely hot to freezing, in just a few hours.This is due to its lack of a significant atmosphere to regulate temperature.

In the microgravity of space, astronauts experience a slight increase in height as their spines decompress. This is a temporary effect, however, and they return to their normal height once they come back to Earth.

Astronauts aboard the International Space Station witness 16 sunrises and sunsets every day due to its high speed and low Earth orbit.

Due to the lack of wind or water on the moon, the footprints left by astronauts during the Apollo missions will likely remain for millions of years. This is a stark reminder of humanity's first steps on another celestial body.

The first pizza was delivered to space in 2001 for astronauts aboard the International Space Station. The pizza was specially prepared to be safe and edible in the space environment.

Orbiting at an altitude of around 250 miles (400 kilometers) above Earth and moving at a tremendous speed of approximately 17,500 miles per hour (28,000 kilometers per hour), it completes a full orbit around our planet about every 90 minutes.

Mars is home to the longest canyon in the solar system, Valles Marineris, which is large enough to fit the Grand Canyon inside it 20 times. This canyon system stretches over 2,500 miles across the Martian surface.

The Milky Way galaxy is home to over 200 billion stars, showcasing the vastness of our galaxy. This number is only an estimate, however, and the actual number could be much higher.

Neutron stars are the extraordinarily dense, collapsed cores left behind after a massive star explodes in a supernova.

A single teaspoon of their material would weigh about as much as a mountain on Earth, showcasing the extreme conditions that exist in these celestial objects.

The flag planted on the moon during the Apollo 11 mission in 1969 still stands, but its colors have faded due to the harsh lunar environment. This flag is a symbol of one of humanity's greatest achievements.

Mars experiences the largest dust storms in our solar system, which can last for months and cover the entire planet. These dust storms can affect the operation of rovers and other equipment on Mars.

The sun's size is so immense that it could hold approximately 1.3 million Earths. This underscores the sun's massive scale and its gravitational dominance in our solar system.

Despite its size, Saturn is light enough that it would float in water if such a scenario were possible. This is because its overall density is less than that of water, a result of its composition primarily of hydrogen and helium.

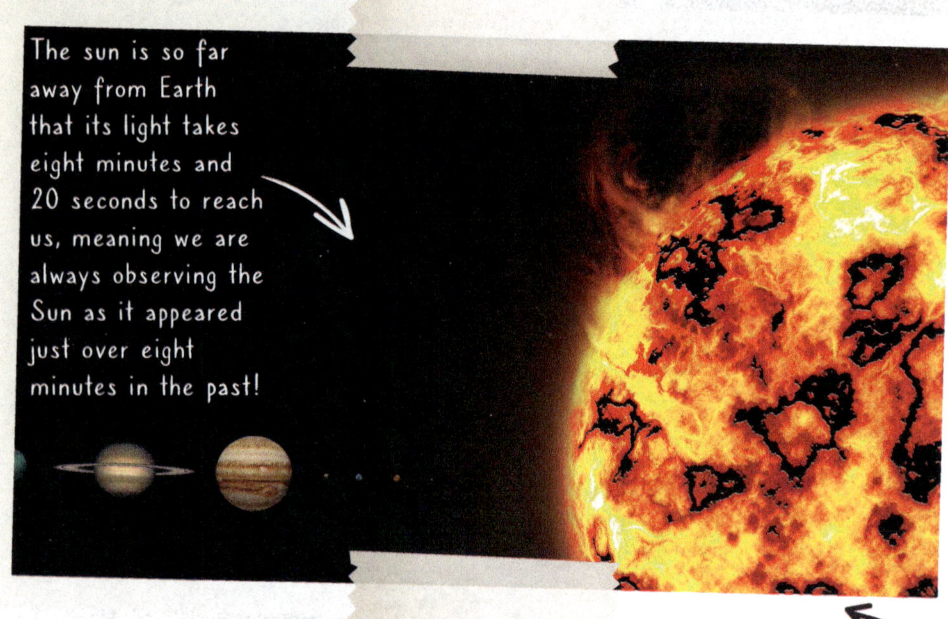

Despite light's incredible speed of approximately 186,282 miles per second (299,791 km per second), if the Sun were to suddenly disappear, we wouldn't know for a little over eight minutes since the last beams of light would still be in transit.

The exoplanet 55 Cancri e is believed to be largely composed of diamond-like crystals. This is due to its high carbon content and extreme pressure and temperature conditions.

Neptune has the strongest winds in our solar system, reaching speeds of up to 1,200 mph (1,931 kph). These extreme winds are driven by the planet's rapid rotation and internal heat.

Some scientists hypothesize the existence of a hidden, giant planet in our solar system, often referred to as Planet Nine. This hypothetical planet, if it exists, would explain certain anomalies in the orbits of some objects in the Kuiper Belt.

Black holes have such intense gravity that nothing, not even light, can escape once it gets too close. This makes them invisible to traditional observation methods, and they can only be detected indirectly.

Our home galaxy, the Milky Way, and our cosmic neighbor, the Andromeda galaxy, are gradually drifting towards a monumental collision, albeit one that won't occur for another approximate 4.5 billion years.

The first living creatures sent to space were fruit flies, launched by the U.S. in 1947 to study the effects of space travel on living organisms. The fruit flies were recovered alive, paving the way for future human space travel.

When they finally do meet, it'll cause lots of new stars to form as gas clouds get squashed together. However, the space between stars is so vast, actual collisions between stars are very unlikely. Eventually, after billions of years, the two galaxies will join together into one larger galaxy.

Jupiter's Great Red Spot, a storm larger than Earth itself, has been continuously active for over 300 years. This storm is a prominent feature of Jupiter's thick, turbulent atmosphere.

On the exoplanet HD 189733b, it's believed that glass rains sideways due to its extreme atmospheric conditions. This is a result of its high temperature and powerful winds, which create an environment vastly different from Earth's.

The Milky Way galaxy is spinning at a speed of about 168 miles (270 km) per second. Despite this fast pace, our galaxy still takes about 200 million years to make one full rotation!

Pluto completes one rotation on its axis about every 6.4 Earth days, meaning a single day on Pluto is about a week on Earth. Also, Pluto and its largest moon, Charon, are tidally locked, which means they always show the same face to each other. From a certain spot on Pluto, Charon would hang motionless in the sky.

Space is completely silent due to the lack of air or any medium to transmit sound waves. This means that astronauts have to rely on radio waves to communicate while in space.

In 2013, astronaut Chris Hadfield recorded the first music video in space, a cover of David Bowie's "Space Oddity". The video was filmed aboard the International Space Station and has been viewed millions of times on Earth.

The dwarf planet Haumea, located beyond Neptune, has an elongated shape and completes a rotation every 3.9 hours. This rapid rotation causes Haumea to have an oblong shape, unlike most other celestial bodies.

In the vacuum of space, two pieces of the same type of metal can bond together permanently if they touch, a phenomenon known as cold welding. This is due to the absence of air and water that would normally form a layer of oxidation on the metal.

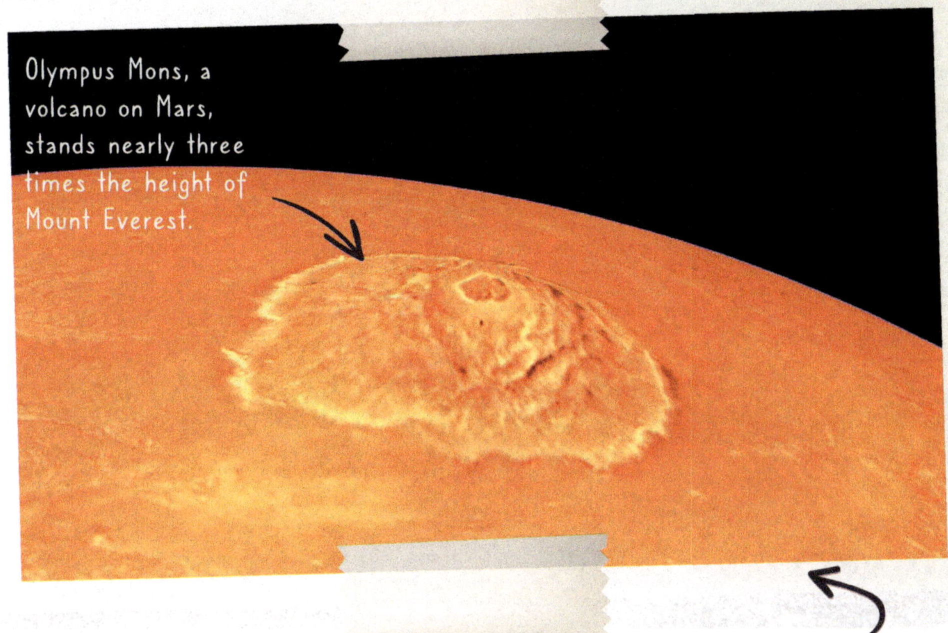

Olympus Mons holds the record for the tallest known mountain in our entire solar system. It reaches an incredible height of about 13.6 miles (22 kilometers), nearly three times the height of Mount Everest, which stands at roughly 5.5 miles (8.8 kilometers) tall.

The International Space Station, the largest man-made object in space, can occasionally be seen from Earth without the use of a telescope. It appears as a bright, fast-moving point of light in the night sky.

A full NASA space suit costs around 12 million dollars, reflecting the complexity and high-tech nature of these suits. These suits are designed to protect astronauts from the harsh conditions of space and provide life support during spacewalks.

If all of the DNA in your body were unraveled, it would stretch from the Earth to the sun and back approximately 600 times. This illustrates the compactness of DNA, which stores the genetic information of all living organisms.

The moon is gradually moving away from Earth at a rate similar to the growth speed of human fingernails. This is due to tidal friction, which also causes the Earth's rotation to slow down over time.

Most meteors completely burn up in the atmosphere, with only a small percentage—those composed of more resilient materials or larger in size—reaching the ground as meteorites.

The speed of light is approximately 186,282 miles per second (299,791 km per second), making it the fastest known speed in the universe. This speed is a fundamental constant of nature and forms the basis of Einstein's theory of relativity.

Astronauts have reported that space has a distinct smell, often described as a mix of hot metal and welding fumes. This smell is likely caused by high-energy vibrations in particles brought inside the spacecraft after spacewalks.

Astronomers have discovered a planet that orbits two stars, like the fictional planet Tatooine in Star Wars. This type of system, known as a circumbinary system, wasonce thought to be purely science fiction.

If you could drive to the moon at a consistent speed of 60 miles per hour (97 kph), it would take about six months to reach it. This gives a sense of the vast distance between Earth and its natural satellite.

DINOSAUR SECRETS

This dinosaur is one of the largest land animals ever to have existed, with some estimates suggesting it could have weighed up to 100 tons. However, Argentinosaurus started life in an egg about the size of a football. This means that these dinosaurs experienced an incredible growth spurt during their life, a testament to the plentiful food and favorable conditions of their environment.

Some dinosaurs, like the Parasaurolophus, had hollow crests on their heads that may have been used to produce sound. These dinosaurs could have used these sounds for communication, similar to how many modern animals use calls or songs.

The Woolly Mammoth, a creature from the Ice Age, was covered in a thick layer of hair. This adaptation helped it survive in the harsh, cold environments of the Pleistocene epoch.

The Dimetrodon was a pre-dinosaur reptile with a sail on its back that helped regulate its body temperature. This creature is often mistaken for a dinosaur, but it actually went extinct before the first dinosaurs appeared.

The Coelacanth, a prehistoric fish thought to be extinct, was rediscovered in 1938. This "living fossil" provides a unique glimpse into the marine life of the distant past.

The Troodon is considered one of the smartest dinosaurs due to its high brain-to-body ratio. This dinosaur's large brain size suggests it may have relied more on its intelligence than on physical strength to survive.

The Tyrannosaurus rex had teeth that were as long as bananas (up to 9 inches or 23 centimeters long), indicating its powerful bite.

Palm trees first appeared around 80 million years ago, during the late Cretaceous period. These trees, which are more closely related to grass than to other tree species, have since spread to tropical and subtropical regions around the world.

These teeth were not only fearsome but also uniquely designed for biting and ripping into flesh, allowing the T. rex to tackle large prey and even other dinosaurs. In fact, studies suggest that the bite force of a T. rex could have been the strongest of any terrestrial animal that has ever lived.

The term "dinosaur" originates from Greek and translates to "terrible lizard." This name was coined by Sir Richard Owen in 1842, reflecting the immense size and power of these prehistoric creatures.

Despite its large body size, the Stegosaurus had a brain that was only about the size of a walnut. This has led scientists to speculate that these dinosaurs relied more on their spiked tails and armored plates for defense than on their intelligence.

The Dunkleosteus, a gigantic prehistoric fish was one of the apex predators of its time, demonstrating the diversity and power of ancient marine life.

DUNKLEOSTEUS
(380 TO 360 MILLION YEARS AGO)

Instead of teeth, Dunkleosteus had two long, bony blades that could snap shut with tremendous force. Scientists estimate that it could open its mouth in just one-fiftieth of a second, creating a strong suction force to pull in its prey. When it closed its mouth, the force was enough to crush armor or break bones.

The Compsognathus, a small and fast dinosaur, likely hunted insects. This dinosaur's small size and agility would have made it an efficient hunter of small prey.

Some dinosaurs had sharp, curved claws that would have aided them in climbing trees. This suggests a level of adaptability and diversity in dinosaur behavior and habitats.

The Hesperornis was a prehistoric diving bird that swam in the ocean and had sharp teeth. This bird is a fascinating example of the diversity of avian life during the age of dinosaurs.

The Eoraptor was one of the earliest known dinosaurs, living around 230 million years ago. This small, bipedal dinosaur was a carnivore, and it provides important clues about the early evolution of dinosaurs.

It was one of the first plants to form forests. Through photosynthesis, Archaeopteris lowered high levels of carbon dioxide and increased oxygen, paving the way for more land-based animal life. Its deep roots also helped form soil and further reduced carbon dioxide. Although extinct, Archaeopteris set the groundwork for the forests we have today.

The Woolly Mammoth, a creature from the Ice Age, had long, curved tusks. These tusks, which could grow up to 15 feet (4.5m) long, were likely used for fighting and foraging through deep snow.

The Titanoboa was a massive snake that could grow up to 40 feet (12 m) long. This prehistoric serpent, which lived after the extinction of the dinosaurs, is the largest snake known to have existed.

The Megaloceros, also known as the Irish Elk, was a giant deer with enormous antlers. Despite its name, it was not actually an elk but was more closely related to modern-day deer.

The Pachycephalosaurus had a thick, bony dome on its head, which may have been used in combat. This dinosaur could have used its head in a ramming attack against predators or rivals.

Many experts believe that a large meteorite struck Mexico's Yucatan Peninsula 65.5 million years ago, causing the extinction of dinosaurs, pterosaurs, and plesiosaurs.

The impact would have sent shockwaves around the world, resulting in a mass extinction where no land animal larger than a big dog survived. Despite this cataclysm, many species, including sharks, jellyfish, fish, scorpions, birds, insects, snakes, turtles, lizards, and crocodiles, managed to survive.

During the Carboniferous Period, giant insects like dragonflies with 2.5-foot (76 cm) wingspans and 8-foot (2.5 m) long millipedes roamed the Earth. The high oxygen levels during this period allowed insects to grow much larger than they do today.

The Compsognathus was a small, fast dinosaur about the size of a chicken. Despite its small size, it was likely a fierce predator, using its speed and agility to catch insects and small vertebrates.

The Dire Wolf was a prehistoric carnivore that lived during the last Ice Age. These wolves were larger and heavier than modern wolves, and they likely hunted large herbivores.

Pterosaurs, flying reptiles that lived during the time of the dinosaurs, were not actually dinosaurs themselves. Despite this, they shared a common ancestor with dinosaurs and are often associated with them.

The Microraptor was a unique dinosaur with four wings.

It had long, feathered arms and legs that functioned like wings, much like the wings you'd see on today's birds. Scientists are still debating whether it truly flew like birds do or if it was more of a glider, using its wings to soar from tree to tree. These ancient four-winged creatures help us understand how flight may have evolved, bridging the gap between birds and non-avian dinosaurs.

The Brachiosaurus had nostrils located on the top of its head. This unique feature, along with its long neck, may have helped it to keep its head cool while feeding on treetops.

The prehistoric shark, Megalodon, had teeth the size of a human hand. This giant predator, which could grow up to 60 feet (18 m) long, was one of the most formidable creatures in the ocean.

The first flowers on Earth emerged around 130 million years ago during the Cretaceous period. This period, also known as the "Age of Dinosaurs," saw a significant diversification of plant life, which in turn supported a variety of herbivorous dinosaurs.

The Ankylosaurus was heavily armored and had a club-like tail for defense. This dinosaur's body was covered in bony plates, and its tail could have been used to strike predators.

The Spinosaurus was larger than the T. rex and had a large sail on its back.

New research suggested that Spinosaurus was a semi-aquatic dinosaur - one of the very few known to scientists. This claim is based on the discovery of a well-preserved Spinosaurus tail, which appears to be adapted for swimming, much like a crocodile's tail. If correct, this would make Spinosaurus one of the most unique dinosaurs, capable of thriving on both land and water.

The Ankylosaurus had a tail resembling a club, which it likely used for defense. This dinosaur was heavily armored, with bony plates covering its back and sides, making it one of the most well-protected creatures of the dinosaur era.

The Maiasaura, a herbivorous dinosaur, is known for its nurturing behavior towards its young. Fossil evidence suggests that Maiasaura parents cared for their offspring in nests, a behavior rarely seen in reptiles.

During the Carboniferous period, Earth's atmosphere had a higher oxygen concentration, which may have allowed for larger insects and arthropods. This period, often referred to as the "Age of Insects," saw the emergence of some of the largest insects in Earth's history.

The Brachiosaurus, known for its long neck, could reach up to 85 feet (26 m) tall. This height, combined with its ability to walk on four legs, allowed it to feed on foliage that other herbivores couldn't reach.

Some dinosaur species, such as the Velociraptor, were feathered, suggesting a close relation to birds.

This discovery also helped reframe our understanding of dinosaurs. They were not all the scale-covered, reptilian-like creatures we once imagined. Many, especially among theropods, had feathers, and looked much more bird-like than lizard-like. This is a dramatic shift that continues to influence paleontology and our comprehension of the evolutionary history of life on Earth.

The largest dinosaur eggs ever discovered were roughly the size of basketballs. These eggs belonged to the sauropod dinosaur group, which includes some of the largest animals to have ever lived.

The first grass appeared on Earth around 66 million years ago during the Cretaceous period. This development had a significant impact on the ecosystem, providing a new food source for many herbivorous dinosaurs.

The Megatherium, also known as the giant ground sloth, was as large as an elephant. This massive mammal, which lived during the Ice Age, is one of the largest land mammals known to have existed.

The Archaeopteryx is considered a crucial link between dinosaurs and birds due to its shared features. This creature had feathers and wings like a bird, but also had teeth and a long, bony tail like a dinosaur.

OCEANIC ODYSSEY

The blue whale, an incredible marine giant reaching lengths of 100 feet (30 meters) and weighing up to 200 tons (181 metric tons), holds the title for the largest animal ever to have lived on Earth, far surpassing even the largest dinosaurs in sheer size.

A blue whale's heart alone is so large that a human could swim through its arteries. Despite their size, these gentlegiants feed mostly on tiny shrimp-like animals called krill, consuming up to 4 tons of krill a day during feeding season.

The Colossal squid possesses the largest beak of any squid species, used to capture and consume prey. This deep-sea dweller is also the largest known invertebrate, with the biggest recorded specimen measuring about 16 feet (4.8 m) long.

The stonefish is the world's most venomous fish, camouflaging itself on the ocean floor to ambush prey. Its dorsal fin spines contain a potent venom that can be fatal to humans if not treated promptly.

The Christmas tree worm gets its name from its colorful, spiral-shaped gills that resemble the branches of a Christmas tree. These marine worms are commonly found on coral reefs and are known for their bright colors.

The narwhal, often referred to as the "unicorn of the sea," is known for its long, spiral tusk. This tusk, which can reach lengths of up to 10 feet (3 m), is actually an elongated tooth and is most commonly found in males.

Sea otters have the densest fur of any animal, with up to 1 million hairs per square inch. This dense fur provides insulation, keeping them warm in the cold waters of the Pacific Ocean.

Some species of shark, such as the hammerhead, have a special organ called the ampullae of Lorenzini that can detect electrical fields.

The Pacific barreleye fish has a transparent head, allowing it to see through its own skull. This unique adaptation allows it to look for prey and predators directly above it in the dimly lit waters of the deep sea.

Their broad, flat heads give them a wide field of electrical detection. This helps them sweep the ocean floor for hidden prey, such as stingrays buried in the sand. This ability, combined with their acute sense of smell, makes sharks incredibly efficient hunters.

Some species of sea turtles, such as the loggerhead, can hold their breath for up to 5 hours. They achieve this by slowing their heart rate to conserve oxygen, with heartbeats dropping to as low as one every nine minutes.

Humpback whales possess the longest flippers of any whale species, reaching up to 16 feet (4.8 m) long. These long flippers, which can be up to a third of their body length, give them increased maneuverability in the water.

The Mariana Trench, located in the western Pacific Ocean, is the deepest part of the world's oceans, reaching a depth of over 36,000 feet (10,973 meters).

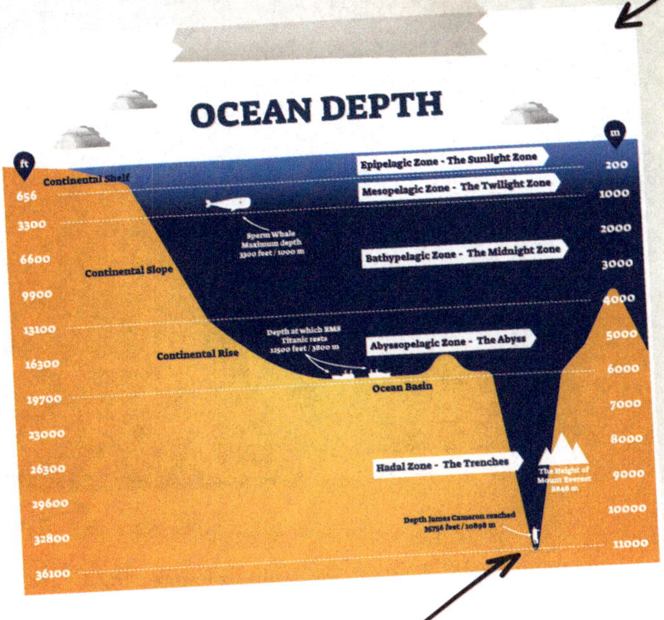

The mantis shrimp has powerful claws that it uses to hunt, capable of striking with the speed of a bullet. This rapid strike is so powerful that it can break glass aquarium walls and is used to crack open the shells of its prey.

With pressures similar to Titan's surface, temperatures echoing the cold of Mars, and an eternal darkness comparable to space's black expanse, the Mariana Trench parallels conditions found on extraterrestrial bodies. The presence of life in such harsh conditions also hints at the potential for life in the extreme environments of other celestial bodies, like the deep oceans speculated to exist on Jupiter's moon Europa or Saturn's moon Enceladus.

The giant squid possesses the largest eyes in the animal kingdom, measuring up to 10 inches (25 cm) in diameter. These enormous eyes help the squid see in the dark depths of the ocean where light is scarce.

The Greenland shark, one of the slowest-moving sharks, has a lifespan that can exceed 400 years. This makes it one of the longest-lived vertebrates on Earth.

Underwater rivers and lakes exist in the ocean, formed by differences in salinity and temperature. These underwater bodies of water, known as brine pools, can be so dense that they form a distinct surface and shoreline, much like a lake or river on land.

This process, called 'transdifferentiation', lets its cells change their function, essentially transforming the jellyfish back into its juvenile form known as a 'polyp'. While this trick allows it to avoid dying of old age, the jellyfish can still be killed by predators or diseases. Nonetheless, this unique ability to hit life's reset button continues to intrigue scientists.

The Great Barrier Reef, located off the coast of Australia, is the largest living structure on Earth and can be seen from space. This massive coral reef system, stretching over 1,400 miles (2,300 kilometers), is home to thousands of marine species and is considered one of the seven natural wonders of the world.

The sawfish has a long, flat snout lined with sharp teeth that it uses to slash through prey. This unique rostrum can also detect the electrical signals of hidden prey in the sand due to the presence of small electroreceptors.

The box jellyfish is one of the most venomous creatures on Earth, posing a significant danger to humans. Its tentacles are lined with thousands of specialized cells called cnidocytes, each containing a tiny, barbed thread that can deliver a potent venom.

The dumbo octopus, named for its ear-like fins, uses these fins to swim in the deep ocean. Living at depths of up to 22,000 feet (7,000 meters), it's one of the deepest dwelling species known to man.

The Portuguese man o' war is not a single organism but a colony of individual organisms called zooids, working together as one.

These different zooids can't exist independently, but when connected, they create a formidable life-form capable of navigating the open ocean, capturing prey, and reproducing. The Portuguese man o' war's unique biological structure is a remarkable example of nature's ingenuity, showing how teamwork and division of labor can lead to survival in the harsh open seas.

The mimic octopus can change its shape, color, and behavior to imitate other sea creatures. This ability helps it to avoid predators and sometimes to lure prey.

Clownfish and sea anemones have a symbiotic relationship, where the clownfish protects the anemone from predators, and the anemone provides the clownfish with a safe home. The clownfish has a layer of mucus on its skin that protects it from the anemone's stinging cells.

Sea cucumbers have a unique defense mechanism where they can eject their internal organs out of their bodies to deter predators. After the threat has passed, they can regenerate these organs in a matter of weeks.

The deep-sea dragonfish uses a bioluminescent lure on its chin to attract prey in the dark ocean depths. This deep-sea predator also has a row of light-producing organs along its belly to camouflage itself from predators below.

Found in many of the world's oceans, they are famous for their gender disparity, with females growing up to 6.6 feet (2 meters) while males only reach a length of about an inch (2.4 cm). This extreme size difference is one of the most pronounced in the animal kingdom.

The leatherback sea turtle is the largest sea turtle, weighing up to 1,500 pounds (680 kg). Unlike other sea turtles, the leatherback lacks a hard, bony shell and instead has a leathery carapace for which it is named.

The vampire squid has large, red eyes and webbed arms that it can use to envelop its prey. Despite its name, it doesn't feed on blood but rather on detritus that falls to the ocean floor, earning it the nickname "garbage collector of the sea."

The deep-sea hatchetfish gets its name from its thin, flat body that resembles the blade of a hatchet. These fish have bioluminescent properties, which they use as a method of counter-illumination to hide their shadows from predators below.

Approximately 70% of Earth's surface is covered by water, primarily in the form of oceans. This vast expanse of water plays a crucial role in regulating the planet's climate and is home to an incredible diversity of life, much of which remains unexplored.

This mass spawning event ensures the survival of the species. Sunfish are among the heaviest of all bony fishes, with adults typically weighing between 545 and 2,205 lbs (247 and 1,000 kg), though larger specimens can reach an incredible 5,070 lbs (2,300 kg). Despite their enormous size, sunfish are harmless to humans and feed mainly on jellyfish, small fishes, plankton, and algae.

The pistol shrimp can create a shockwave capableof stunning its prey by snapping its claw shut at high speed. This action creates a bubble that, when it collapses, produces a sound loud enough to stun or even kill small fish.

The ribbon eel can change its color and sex during its lifetime. All ribbon eels start their lives as males, with black bodies and a yellow dorsal fin, and as they mature, they change color and become females.

Some fish, like the anglerfish, have evolved unique hunting mechanisms, such as a built-in lure on their heads to attract prey. This bioluminescent appendage mimics smaller prey, luring unsuspecting fish and squid into the anglerfish's mouth.

The electric eel is capable of generating an electric shock of up to 600 volts to stun prey and deter predators. Despite its name, it's not actually an eel but a type of knifefish.

They use their sharp beak to snatch fish from the water, and a unique system of backward-facing spines on their upper palate and tongue helps hold the fish in place. These spines work like a ratchet, preventing the fish from sliding out while the puffin opens its beak to catch more fish.

In seahorse species, it is the male that becomes pregnant and gives birth to the offspring. The female deposits her eggs into a special pouch on the male's belly, where he fertilizes and carries them until they are ready to hatch.

Coral reefs are composed of millions of tiny animals called coral polyps, which build the reef's structure over thousands of years. These "rainforests of the sea" are some of the most biodiverse ecosystems on Earth, providing a home for a large variety of marine life.

The Pacific Ocean is the largest ocean on Earth, spanning more area than all of Earth's landmass combined. It's so vast that it contains more than half of the world's free water and is larger than the total land area of every continent combined.

The frilled shark has over 300 teeth arranged in 25 rows. This deep-sea dweller is often referred to as a "living fossil" due to its primitive features and the fact that it has changed little over millions of years.

INGENIOUS INVENTIONS

The first airplane was invented by the Wright brothers, Orville and Wilbur, who made their first successful flight on December 17, 1903 in Kitty Hawk, North Carolina.

The first flight, piloted by Orville, covered 120 feet (36 meters) in 12 seconds. They managed four flights that day, the longest being 852 feet (260 meters) in 59 seconds, a modest beginning to an era of human flight.

The first microwave oven was invented in 1946 by Percy Spencer, an engineer at the Raytheon Corporation, who discovered the cooking potential of microwaves when a candy bar in his pocket melted.

The first potato chips were invented by George Crum in 1853, a chef in Saratoga Springs, New York, who was trying to appease a customer who complained that his fries were too thick.

The first bicycle, known as a "running machine" or "dandy horse," was invented by Karl von Drais in 1817. It didn't have pedals, and the rider pushed it along with their feet.

The first digital camera was invented in 1975 by Steven Sasson, an engineer at Eastman Kodak. It weighed 8 pounds (3.6 kg) and took 23 seconds to capture a single image.

The first rubber eraser was invented in 1770 by Edward Nairne, an English engineer.

The first recipe for popcorn is found in a Peruvian tomb believed to be over 6,700 years old. The kernels found in the tomb were so well preserved that they could still pop.

The first 3D movie, "The Power of Love," was released in 1922, and viewers had to wear anaglyph glasses (red/green or red/blue lenses) to see the 3D effects.

The first chocolate bar was invented in 1847 by Joseph Fry, who discovered that he could make a moldable chocolate paste by adding melted cacao butter back into Dutch cocoa.

The first crayons were invented by Edwin Binney and C. Harold Smith, who owned a paint company called Binney & Smith, which later became Crayola.

These glasses, with their red and green or red and blue lenses, allowed each eye to see a slightly different image, creating the illusion of depth and making the scenes appear three-dimensional. This was an early form of the 3D technology we are familiar with today.

The first modern trampoline was invented in 1936 by George Nissen and Larry Griswold. They were both gymnasts and wanted to use the trampoline to train tumblers.

The first solar-powered calculator was invented in 1978 by Sharp Corporation. It was called the EL-8026, and it had a solar cell that powered the calculator in addition to a battery.

The first roller coaster was built in 1884 at Coney Island in New York was inspired by the old mining railroads that were once used to shuttle coal down mountains.

It was simple compared to today's high-tech roller coasters. It consisted of two wooden tracks that dropped 600 feet (183 m) at a gentle 6 mph (10 kph). Passengers would climb to the top of a platform and ride along the track in a car, then switch to another car to return to the start.

The first practical refrigerator was invented in 1913 by Fred W. Wolf of Fort Wayne, Indiana. It was called the "DomeIre," or DOMestic ELectric REfrigerator.

The first vacuum cleaner was invented in 1901 by Hubert Cecil Booth. The machine, called the "Puffing Billy," was powered by an engine and had to be pulled by horses.

The first mechanical clock was invented in China in the 8th century by a Buddhist monk and mathematician named Yi Xing.

The first zippers were invented in 1893 by Whitcomb Judson, who intended them to be used for shoes.

The first television was invented in the 1920s by John Logie Baird. Early televisions were mechanical and had a spinning disk with holes to create the image.

The first metal detector was invented in 1881 by Alexander Graham Bell. He created it to find a bullet lodged in President James Garfield after an assassination attempt.

The first pair of eyeglasses was invented in Italy around 1290, though the inventor is unknown.

They used a spinning disk with holes in it that would scan a picture, line by line. The light from the picture would then hit a sensor that turned this light into an electrical signal. This signal was then sent to another device that could recreate the picture. This basic technology was the beginning of the TV as we know it today.

The first version of the internet, ARPANET (Advanced Research Projects Agency Network), was developed in the late 1960s and early 1970s by the U.S. Department of Defense.

The first vending machine was invented by Hero of Alexandria, a Greek engineer, in the first century. It dispensed holy water when a coin was inserted.

The first email was sent in 1971 by Ray Tomlinson, an American computer programmer. He used the "@" symbol to separate the user's name from the computer's name.

The first mobile phone call was made in 1973 by Martin Cooper, a Motorola executive, who made the call on a Motorola DynaTAC, a device that weighed 2.2 pounds (1 kg).

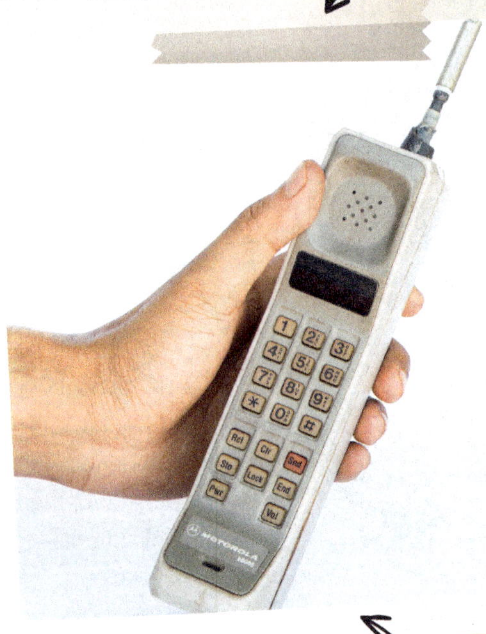

The first skateboard was created in the 1950s in California by surfers who wanted to "surf" on land when the waves were flat.

The first commercial jigsaw puzzle was created in 1908 by Archie McPhee. It was called the "Jig of the Century" and had 500 pieces.

It could only be used for 30 minutes before it needed to be charged again, and charging took a long 10 hours! Even though it took ten more years for this phone to be sold to the public, its invention in 1973 changed everything. It showed a future where people could talk to each other from anywhere, not just from home or work.

The first traffic light was installed outside the Houses of Parliament in London in 1868. It was gas-lit and manually operated by a police officer.

The ice cream cone was popularized during the 1904 World's Fair in St. Louis, Missouri, where an ice cream vendor ran out of dishes and partnered with a nearby waffle vendor to serve his ice cream in a rolled-up waffle.

The first electric toaster was invented in 1893 by George Schneider and Albert Marsh. It was called the "Eclipse" and could toast only one side of the bread at a time.

The first photocopier, called the Xerox 914, was invented in 1959 by Chester Carlson. It was a dry process called xerography that used electrostatic charges on a light-sensitive photoreceptor to attract and hold toner particles, which were then transferred onto paper and fused with heat.

The ice cream cone was popularized during the 1904 World's Fair in St. Louis, Missouri, where an ice cream vendor ran out of dishes and partnered with a nearby waffle vendor to serve his ice cream in a rolled-up waffle.

The first recorded use of toilet paper dates back to the 6th century in China. However, it wasn't until the 14th century that it started being mass-produced.

The first electric iron was invented in 1882 by Henry W. Seeley. It was called the "electric flatiron" and made ironing clothes a breeze!

It was an instant hit, providing a convenient, edible container that patrons could munch on after they finished their ice cream, leaving no waste. This simple yet brilliant innovation transformed the way ice cream was served and enjoyed, quickly spreading globally. Today, it's hard to imagine enjoying a scoop of ice cream without the iconic cone.

The first rubber band was invented in 1845 by Stephen Perry, a British inventor. They were originally made from vulcanized rubber and used to hold papers or envelopes together.

The first electric blender was invented in 1922 by Stephen Poplawski. He wanted to make it easier to mix malted milk drinks.

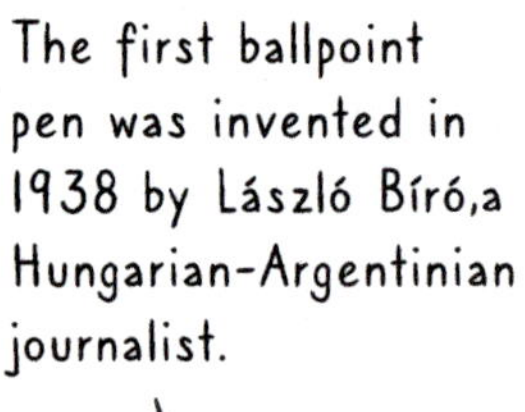

The first ballpoint pen was invented in 1938 by László Bíró, a Hungarian-Argentinian journalist.

He designed a tiny ball bearing in the tip of the pen that was free to turn around. As you write, the ball spins and draws ink from the cartridge onto the paper. This means the ink dries quickly and doesn't smudge. Bíró's invention was a huge success and even today, we still use 'biros' for everyday writing!

The first chewing gum was invented in 1848 by John B. Curtis. It was made from the sap of the spruce tree and called "State of Maine Pure Spruce Gum."

The first traffic cones were invented in 1940 by Charles D. Scanlon, an American painter. They were originally made of wood and used to keep cars away from wet paint.

The first recorded recipe for s'mores dates back to 1927 in a Girl Scouts guidebook. The guidebook, titled "Tramping and Trailing with the Girl Scouts," included a recipe for "Some More" which was later shortened to "S'mores."

The first automatic dishwasher was invented in 1886 by Josephine Cochrane, a wealthy socialite who was tired of her dishes being chipped by her servants. She showcased her invention at the 1893 World's Fair in Chicago and won the highest prize for "best mechanical construction, durability and adaptation to its line of work."

The first escalator was invented in 1891 by Jesse W. Reno. It was called the "inclined elevator" and was used as an amusement park ride.

Reno's design was quite different from today's escalators. Instead of steps, it had a slanted, moving platform with a non-slip texture. People would stand on this platform and be carried upwards. It was an instant hit, and later, engineers modified and improved Reno's design to make the modern, stepped escalator we all use today. So, next time you're on an escalator, remember it started as a fun ride at a fair!

The first electric blender was invented in 1922 by Stephen Poplawski. He wanted to make it easier to mix malted milk drinks, but the blender has since been used to make everything from smoothies to soups.

The first disposable diaper was invented in 1947 by Marion Donovan. It was called the "Boater" and was made of waterproof plastic.

The first electric washing machine was invented in 1908 by Alva J. Fisher. It was called the "Thor" and looked like a large wooden barrel.

The first video game, "Tennis for Two," was invented in 1958 by William Higinbotham, a physicist at the Brookhaven National Laboratory.

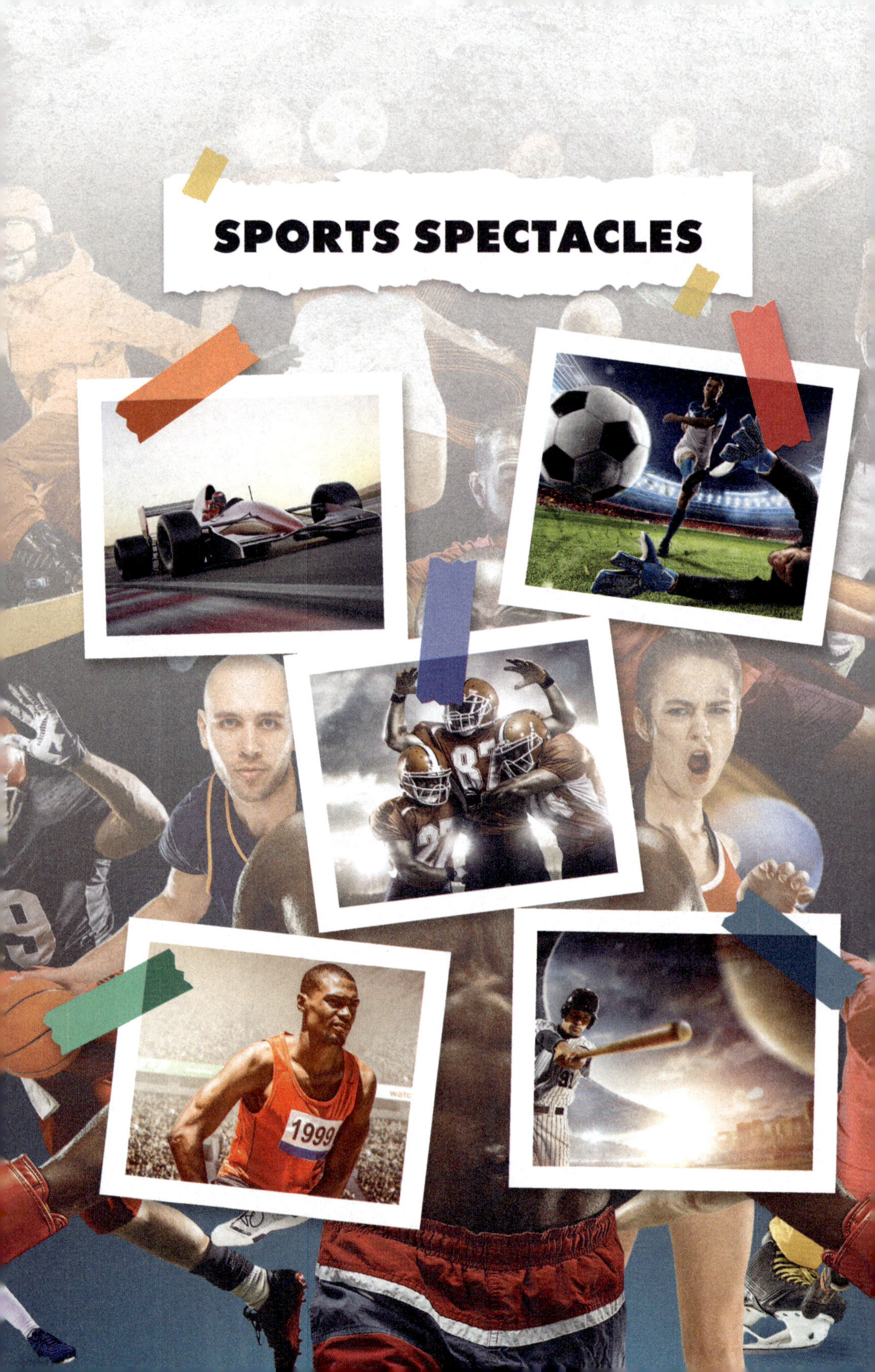
SPORTS SPECTACLES
1999

This large quantity is due to a variety of factors, including the potential for balls to be kicked into the stands, damaged during play, or taken out of play for inspection if a team challenges the amount of air inside.

Aroldis Chapman, a Cuban-American professional baseball pitcher, holds the record for the fastest baseball pitch, clocking in at 105.1 mph (169.1 kph). This record was set in 2010 when Chapman was playing for the Cincinnati Reds against the San Diego Padres.

Senet, a game from ancient Egypt around 3100 BCE, is the world's oldest known board game. The game was played on a grid of 30 squares arranged in three rows of ten and involved moving pieces based on the roll of a dice.

The record for the largest game of dodgeball was set in 2012 with 6,084 participants. The University of California, Irvine organized the event, breaking their own previous record.

Jacob "Baby Jake" Matlala, standing at just 4 feet 10 inches tall (147 cm), was the shortest professional boxer in history. Despite his size, Matlala had a successful career, winning several world championship titles.

Soccer, also known as football, is played by an estimated 270 million people worldwide. This includes both professional players and amateurs, making it the most popular sport globally.

In Spain in 2016, the largest human pyramid was created with 1,202 participants. The event was organized by the Castellers de Vilafranca, a cultural association that builds human towers as a Catalonian tradition.

The longest tennis match in history occurred at Wimbledon in 2010, lasting 11 hours and 5 minutes. The match was played over three days between John Isner and Nicolas Mahut, with Isner eventually winning.

The highest score in a single game of bowling is 300 points, achieved by bowling 12 consecutive strikes. This perfect score is a rare feat, requiring both skill and luck.

The tradition, common in Catalonia, involves people climbing onto each other's shoulders to form tall, tower-like structures. The practice symbolizes unity and teamwork in Catalan culture and is celebrated with music and festivities.

The fastest recorded serve in tennis was hit by Samuel Groth at a speed of 163.7 mph (263.4 kph). This record was set during a Challenger event in Busan, South Korea, in 2012.

Chess, a game that originated in India around the 6th century, is played worldwide today. The game is a two-player strategy board game played on a checkered gameboard with 64 squares arranged in an 8×8 grid.

The highest tightrope walk took place at an altitude of 11,669 feet (3,557 m) above sea level in the French Alps by Freddy Nock from Switzerland in 2015.

Between the two peaks, Freddy walked a tightrope a total of 1,138 ft (347-meter). Freddy did not wear a safety belt, despite the fact that there was a 3280 ft (1,000-meter) drop from the tightrope to the ground below.

In 1989, the largest game of musical chairs involved 8,238 participants. The event took place in Singapore and was organized by the Singapore Sports Council.

In 2016, the largest game of capture the flag involved 2,888 participants achieved by the University of California, Irvine, in California, USA, on September 22, 2015

The longest soccer game lasted for 108 hours and 2 minutes in Scotland in 2019. The match was organized by the charity organization, Scotty's Little Soldiers, and involved 112 players.

There are just two days a year when no professional sports games are played. This is the day before and after the Major League Baseball All-Star Game.

Golf balls can be hit at impressive speeds of up to 170 mph (approximately 274 kph). This speed is largely due to the strength and technique of the golfer, along with the design of the golf club and ball.

For instance, Tiger Woods, one of the most successful golfers of all time, has an average swing speed of around 120 mph (193 kph). His powerful swings, coupled with expert technique, allow him to drive the ball impressive distances. Swing speed is a critical aspect of golf as it directly influences the ball's trajectory, distance, and overall success of a shot.

The largest game of tag involved 10,908 participants in 2019. It was hosted by Fischer's, a YouTube channel with more than 5.8 million subscribers.

The highest score in a game of Scrabble is 830 points. This record was set by Michael Cresta in 2006 during a game in Massachusetts, USA.

In 2007, the largest game of Simon Says involved 12,215 participants at the Utah Summer Games Opening Ceremony in Cedar City, Utah on June 14, 2007.

The largest game of Twister was played on a gargantuan mat that stretched 171 feet 3 inches by 158 feet 5.5 inches (52.19 meters x 48.29 meters). This enormous game sprang to life at the AT&T Stadium in Arlington, Texas.

Usain Bolt, the Jamaican sprinter, reached a speed of 27.8 mph (44.7 kph) during the 100-meter (328-ft) sprint at the 2009 World Championships in Berlin, the fastest recorded sprint speed.

Basketball was invented by a Canadian physical education instructor named James Naismith in December 1891 and was made out of a soccer ball and two peach baskets.

There was no hole in the bottom of these baskets, so whenever someone scored a goal, someone had to climb up and retrieve the ball. Naismith wrote down the basic rules of the game, including dribbling and passing, and nailed this document to the gym wall. The game caught on quickly and evolved over time to become the sport we know today.

The biggest game of leapfrog took place with 1,348 eager school kids at the Canterbury A&P Show in Christchurch, New Zealand on November 11, 2010.

New Zealand's Veronica Torr raced through the 100-meter (328-ft) hurdles in just 18.523 seconds while wearing swim fins. She set this record in Beijing, China, on the set of Zheng Da Zong Yi-Guinness World Records Special on December 8, 2010.

Wilt Chamberlain, an American professional basketball player, scored the highest score in a professional basketball game, with 100 points in 1962. This record was set while playing for the Philadelphia Warriors in a game against the New York Knicks.

Joe Malone, a Canadian professional ice hockey player, scored the most goals in a single ice hockey game by one player, with 7 goals in 1920. This record was set while playing for the Quebec Bulldogs in the National Hockey League.

The longest golf drive was made by Mike Austin in 1974, with the ball traveling 515 yards (470 m). This record was set during the U.S. National Seniors Open Championship in Las Vegas.

Horse racing dates back to roughly 4500 BC, when Central Asian nomadic tribes raced the horses for competitive enjoyment. The Greeks didn't start racing horse-drawn chariots or two-wheeled carts until later in 1000 BC.

Serbian water polo player Aleksander Sapic holds the record for the most goals scored in a single Water Polo World League season, with a staggering 56 goals during the 2005 edition.

The biggest Rock, Paper, Scissors contest ever recorded included 10,033 players. It was organized by Tianjin Joy City in Tianjin, China, from December 21 to 24, 2019, as a part of their 8th-anniversary celebrations.

Eventually, in 664 BC during the 33rd Olympiad, horse racing became an official sport and the riders were called jockeys, just like today. The Romans then introduced horse racing to Britain, and the sport has been popular ever since. So next time you see a horse race, remember it's been around for over 6000 years!

Wasilja Peterse from the Netherlands holds the record for toppling the most mini dominoes - a whopping 3,202 of them! This achievement took place in Arnhem, Gelderland, Netherlands on September 15, 2020, inspired by a domino show on TV back in 1999.

The largest game of hide-and-seek involved 1,437 participants in 2010. The event was organized by the Jiangsu Broadcasting Corporation in Nanjing, China.

Soccer (Football) as we know it today has its roots in an ancient Chinese game called 'cuju'. Played during the Han Dynasty over 2,000 years ago, cuju involved scoring goals by kicking a leather ball through two closely set bamboo canes.

Players kicked a leather ball, but they aimed it between two bamboo canes. These canes were pretty close together, only about 11 to 16 inches (30 to 40 cm) apart. That's about the width of a large computer monitor!

Hasbro, the makers of Monopoly, claim that the longest recorded game stretched on for an incredible 70 days. Unfortunately, the specifics of this marathon gaming session - such as when and where it took place - are lost to history!

On July 25, 2010, the record for the largest space hopper race was set with 771 participants. This bouncy event took place at the Don Valley Grass Bowl in Sheffield, England, UK.

From August 22 to August 25, 2019, Dr. Brent Saik and 55 of his friends in Sherwood Park, Alberta, Canada, set the record for the longest marathon playing baseball. They played for an incredible 83 hours and 13 minutes.

The University of California, Irvine - ASUCI, set the record for the largest game of red light / green light on September 21, 2022, in Irvine, California, USA. A staggering 1,415 participants took part, with the school's mascot, Peter the Anteater, acting as the traffic light.

Before baseball became America's pastime, it was actually first played in England as far back as the 1700s.

The game we know today has its roots in old English village games like rounders and stoolball. These bat-and-ball games, similar to cricket, were used by adults to pass the time, but soon became popular with kids. When the games crossed the Atlantic and reached North America, they evolved and grew in popularity, eventually becoming the sport of baseball. In 1845, Alexander Cartwright in New York City even wrote down rules to formalize the game.

Barry Bonds holds the record for the most home runs in both a single season and throughout his career. In 2001, he broke Mark McGwire's single-season record by hitting 73 home runs. Then, he set the career record by smashing 762 home runs, surpassing Hank Aaron's previous record of 755.

The inaugural Daytona 500 race took place on February 22nd, 1959. Interestingly, it took an entire 61 hours to determine the winner due to an extremely close photo finish. The victory was finally awarded to Lee Petty, who would go on to become the father of the famous race car driver, Richard Petty. This marked the beginning of the Daytona 500's rich history.

CUISINE CHRONICLES

Ostriches, the largest birds on Earth, lay the biggest eggs of any bird species. Their eggs are huge, each one roughly the size of a cantaloupe and weighing as much as 3 pounds! Inside, there's enough space to fit the contents of about 24 chicken eggs.

Chili peppers contain a chemical compound called capsaicin, which binds to pain receptors in your mouth, creating the sensation of burning. This is the same response your body has to physical heat, which is why spicy foods can feel painfully hot.

Although water itself doesn't expire, the plastic bottles it's stored in do have a shelf life and can leach chemicals into the water over time. So, the expiration date you see on bottled water is actually for the bottle, not the water.

Raspberries, known for their sweet-tart flavor, are a member of the Rosaceae family, which also includes roses, strawberries, and apples. This wide-ranging family consists of more than 2,000 species.

Lobsters, now considered a luxury item, were once seen as food for the poor and used as prison food in the colonial era due to their abundance. Over time, as the lobster population declined and transportation improved, lobsters became the delicacy we know today.

If coriander, also known as cilantro, tastes like soap to you, it could be due to a genetic variant in a group of genes that influences the perception of smell and taste. This phenomenon affects approximately 4-14% of the population, depending on ethnic background.

American cheese, often found in the form of rubbery, yellow slices, isn't technically real cheese.

It's made from a blend of Colby and Cheddar cheeses, milk, and various additives and colorings. Its consistency allows it to melt well, and it's valued for its protein and calcium content, even if it's labeled as "American singles" instead of "cheese".

Honey is an incredibly durable food that will never spoil under normal conditions due to its low moisture content and acidic pH. Archaeologists have even found pots of honey in ancient Egyptian tombs that are over 3000 years old and still perfectly edible.

Certain processed foods such as ranch dressing or coffee creamer contain titanium dioxide, a whitening agent also found in paints, plastics, and sunscreens. This compound is used in food to enhance their appearance and make them more appealing.

The red food dye used in Skittles, known as carmine or cochineal, is made from the crushed bodies of a particular type of beetle. This dye has been used as a coloring agent for centuries and is found in a variety of food and cosmetic products.

Pineapple plants, which produce only one fruit at a time, can take two to three years to produce a fruit.

A single pineapple plant can keep producing fruits over a span of up to 50 years. So while they might be slow, these plants are also quite tenacious, continuing to offer up their sweet, tangy fruits for half a century!

The classic pound cake gets its name from its simple recipe: a pound each of flour, butter, eggs, and sugar. This baking tradition dates back to 18th century Europe and was adopted in the Americas due to its simplicity and memorable ingredient ratios.

Nutella, a beloved chocolate-hazelnut spread, consumes about a quarter of the world's hazelnut supply. This heavy reliance on hazelnuts by the Ferrero company, the maker of Nutella, has significant influence on global hazelnut prices.

Farm-raised salmon is naturally greyish-white in color and then dyed pink to match consumer expectations. The pink color in wild salmon comes from their diet of crustaceans, which is not part of the diet of farm-raised salmon.

The color of natural honey can range from light, almost translucent hues to deep, dark browns. This variation is due to the type of flowers the bees visit for nectar, as different flower species contain different pigments which color the honey.

Tomatoes were erroneously believed to be poisonous by Europeans in the 18th century and earned the nickname "the poison apple."

The aristocracy, who ate from pewter plates, often fell ill after eating tomatoes due to the acidic fruit causing lead from the plates to leach into their food, causing lead poisoning. The tomato was wrongly blamed for these ill effects.

The inside of a banana peel can be used to alleviate the itching from a mosquito bite. This relief comes from natural oils present in the peel, which have anti-inflammatory properties.

White chocolate isn't actually chocolate because it lacks cocoa solids, a primary component of traditional chocolate. Instead, it's made from cocoa butter, milk solids, and sugar, which give it a creamy texture and sweet taste.

Despite their name, French fries are believed to have originated in Belgium, where locals had a tradition of deep-frying small fish. When rivers froze in winter and fish were scarce, they cut potatoes into long thin shapes and fried them, leading to what we now call French fries.

Ketchup, in the 1800s, was marketed as a medicinal cure for ailments such as diarrhea, indigestion, and jaundice. This was mainly due to the presence of tomatoes which were believed to have health benefits.

Chicken wings were often discarded or used for making stock until the creation of Buffalo wings in the 1960s by Teressa Bellissimo, owner of the Anchor Bar in Buffalo, New York.

Genetically, around 60% of human genes have counterparts in the banana, demonstrating our shared evolutionary history. Despite this, the traits those genes govern are often quite different between humans and bananas.

The Popsicle was inadvertently invented in 1905 by an 11-year-old boy named Frank Epperson. He left a mixture of powdered soda and water with a stirring stick outside overnight, and it froze, creating the first Popsicle.

This tasty dish, typically served with celery and blue cheese or ranch dressing, involves frying the wings without breading and then coating them in a vinegar-based hot sauce. It quickly caught on, becoming a staple at bars, restaurants, and parties across the country. This tasty invention essentially redefined American snacking culture and solidified the chicken wing as a go-to appetizer and party food.

Despite its longstanding history of vodka consumption, Russia only officially classified beer as an alcoholic beverage in 2011. Before this, beer and any alcoholic beverages under 10% alcohol were considered foodstuffs.

Apple pie, despite being considered a classic American dessert, actually has its origins in Europe. English, Dutch, and Swedish recipes for apple pie date back to hundreds of years before the founding of the United States.

Surprisingly, crackers can contribute to cavities faster than candy. The starch in crackers converts into sugar faster and sticks to teeth longer than sugars from candy. It's the acidic byproduct from this conversion, not sugar itself, that is the primary cause of tooth decay.

Thomas Jefferson, the third U.S. president, is often credited with popularizing pasta in America.

After spending time in Paris, he brought back the first macaroni machine to the U.S., and even designed a pasta machine himself. Jefferson's introduction of mac and cheese has left a lasting impact on American cuisine.

Brussels sprouts, despite being commonly disliked for their distinctive flavor, are among the most nutritious vegetables. They're packed with antioxidants, fiber, vitamins K and C, and have been associated with numerous health benefits.

Almost every banana consumed worldwide is a clone of the Cavendish variety, propagated through a method called vegetative reproduction. This process makes bananas consistently the same in taste and appearance but leaves them vulnerable to diseases.

The Aztecs used cacao beans, the primary ingredient in chocolate, as a form of currency. They were highly valued due to the labor-intensive process required to grow and process them into chocolate.

Black pepper was a luxury item during the Middle Ages, often being referred to as "black gold."

The high demand and significant value of black pepper led to the Age of Discovery in the 15th and 16th centuries, a period marked by global exploration as Europeans sought to establish direct trade routes to India, where black pepper was grown.

Carrots can taste sweeter in the winter as they increase their sugar content to prevent freezing. The added sugar lowers the freezing point inside the cells, acting as a natural antifreeze and thus preventing damage from ice crystals.

Contrary to common belief, Caesar salad isn't Italian but was invented by restaurateur Caesar Cardini in Tijuana, Mexico, in 1927. It was an improvised dish Cardini created during the Fourth of July rush using what he had left in his kitchen.

One burger patty can contain meat from hundreds of different cows due to the processing and mixing techniques used in slaughterhouses. This can make tracing the source of foodborne illnesses more complex.

Doughnuts are named after a practical baking technique pioneered by Elizabeth Gregory. To prevent the dough from undercooking in the center, she inserted nuts into the middle of the dough before frying - thus, they were called dough-nuts.

Potatoes can absorb and reflect radio wave signals (like Wi-Fi signals) similar to the way people do.

When Boeing wanted to improve their in-flight wireless connectivity in 2012, they filled seats with sacks of potatoes to simulate human bodies. The project, humorously named Synthetic Personnel Using Dielectric Substitution (SPUDS), allowed them to test and enhance Wi-Fi signals in various aircraft models.

Pineapple contains an enzyme called bromelain that breaks down proteins. If you feel a tingling or burning sensation in your mouth when eating pineapple, it's because you're extra sensitive to bromelain, which is essentially starting to digest the proteins in your mouth and on your tongue.

Healthy foods, such as fresh fruits, vegetables, and lean proteins, can cost up to 10 times as much as junk foods like fast food or prepackaged meals. This cost difference can be a significant barrier to individuals trying to maintain a balanced diet.

LANDMARK LEGENDS

There's a small town in Norway called "Hell," and it experiences freezing temperatures during the winter months.

The name "Hell" actually comes from the Old Norse word "hellir," which means "overhang" or "cliff cave." It has nothing to do with the English term relating to the underworld. But that doesn't stop English-speaking visitors from chuckling about the chilly weather in "Hell."

Capela dos Ossos is a chapel in Portugal known for its interior walls decorated with human skulls and bones. The chapel was built in the 16th century by a Franciscan monk who wanted to transmit the message of life being transitory.

The Chocolate Hills are a geological formation in the Bohol province of the Philippines. There are at least 1,260 hills, which turn brown during the dry season, giving them their name.

Venice, Italy, is a city built on more than 100 small islands in a lagoon in the Adriatic Sea. With no roads, only canals, it's often referred to as "The Floating City."

Mount Everest, located in the Himalayas, is the highest mountain above sea level. Its peak stands at 29,029 feet (8,848 meters), making it a challenging and popular destination for climbers from around the world.

The world's largest beaver dam, located in Wood Buffalo National Park, Canada, is over 2788 ft (850 m) long. It's so large that it can be seen from space.

The Amazon Rainforest is so dense that when it rains, it can take up to 10 minutes for the water to reach the ground.

The Grand Prismatic Spring in Yellowstone National Park, USA, is the third largest hot spring in the world. It's known for its striking coloration, which is caused by pigmented bacteria in the microbial mats that grow around the edges of the mineral-rich water.

Pig Beach is an uninhabited island located in Exuma, the Bahamas. It's known for its colony of feral pigs that swim freely in the clear waters and interact with tourists.

This delayed trickle-down effect creates multiple microhabitats within the rainforest, each with different moisture levels, temperatures, and light conditions. This diversity supports a vast range of species and contributes to the Amazon's reputation as one of the most biodiverse places on Earth.

The Sahara Desert is the largest hot desert in the world. Covering an area of 3.6 million square miles (9.3 million square km) across several countries in North Africa, it's comparable to the size of the United States.

The Colosseum in Rome, Italy, is the largest amphitheater ever built. Capable of holding an estimated 50,000 to 80,000 spectators, it was used for gladiatorial contests, public spectacles, and dramas.

Vatican City, an independent city-state enclaved within Rome, Italy, is the smallest country in the world by both area and population. It's so small that it could fit inside Central Park in New York City.

Central Park spans about 843 acres, making it nearly eight times larger than Vatican City. Covering just about 110 acres (44 hectares), or 0.17 square miles, it's the smallest internationally recognized independent state in the world. The city-state is home to about 800 residents, far less than many small towns!

The Great Sphinx of Giza in Egypt is one of the world's largest and oldest statues, measuring 241 feet (73 meters) in length and 66 feet (20 meters) in height. Featuring the body of a lion and the head of a human, it was constructed during the reign of Pharaoh Khafre in the Old Kingdom, around 4,500 years ago.

The Eiffel Tower, located in Paris, France, is one of the most recognizable structures in the world. It was initially criticized by some of France's leading artists and intellectuals for its design, but it has become a global cultural icon of France and one of the most visited paid monuments in the world.

The Bermuda Triangle, located in the western part of the North Atlantic Ocean, is famous for the mysterious disappearances of ships and airplanes.

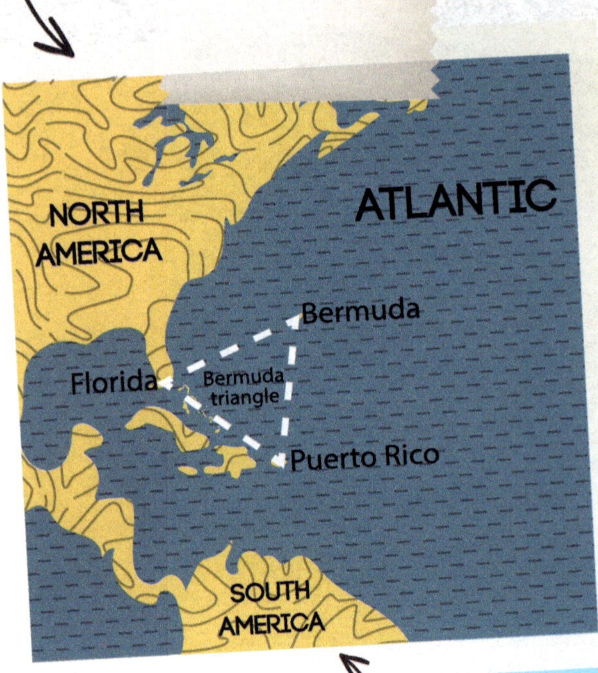

Despite popular beliefs of paranormal activity or alien interventions, most scientists attribute these disappearances to natural geographic and meteorological phenomena.

Nowhere Else is a small rural community in Tasmania, Australia. Its unusual name has made it a point of interest and a popular spot for quirky photo opportunities.

Lake Victoria, located in East Africa, is the largest lake in Africa and the second-largest freshwater lake in the world. It's so large, it could hold enough water to fill everyone's bathtub on Earth.

Eisriesenwelt, located in Austria, is the world's largest ice cave. It extends more than 26 miles (42km), with the first mile (1.6 km) covered in ice.

Istanbul, Turkey, uniquely straddles two continents: Europe and Asia, thanks to its strategic location. This unique position is made possible by the Bosphorus Strait that divides the city into two distinct parts. As a result, residents and visitors can enjoy the extraordinary experience of being in two continents at the very same time, a feature that sets Istanbul apart.

Florida is the flattest state in the U.S., with its highest point, Britton Hill, standing only 345 feet (105 m)above sea level. This makes the landscape of Florida even flatter than a pancake.

Methuselah, a bristlecone pine tree in California's White Mountains, is like a living time capsule. Estimated to be over 4,800 years old, it is among the oldest known non-clonal trees on Earth, comparable to the age of the Great Pyramids of Giza.

The tree's yearly growth rings act as a natural logbook, recording over four millennia of environmental changes. This ancient bristlecone pine, capable of withstanding severe weather conditions and warding off pests with its dense, resinous wood. The specific location of Methuselah is a well-kept secret to protect it from potential harm, similar to precious archaeological sites.

The Galápagos Islands, located in the Pacific Ocean, are home to a species of tortoise that can live for over 150 years. These islands are famous for their unique and diverse wildlife, which inspired Charles Darwin's theory of evolution.

Saint-Louis-du-Ha! Ha! in Quebec, Canada, is the only town in the world with two exclamation points in its name. This unique name reflects the town's vibrant and lively spirit.

Angel Falls in Venezuela is the world's highest uninterrupted waterfall. With a height of 3,212 ft (979 meters) and a plunge of 2,648 ft (807 meters), it's one of the most spectacular sights in the South American country.

Giethoorn is a village in the Dutch province of Overijssel, known for its numerous waterways and lack of roads. The village is often referred to as the "Dutch Venice" due to its many canals and charming thatched-roof houses.

The Taal Volcano in the Philippines is the world's smallest active volcano. Despite its small size, it's one of the most active volcanoes in the Philippines, with 33 recorded eruptions.

The Dead Sea, located between Jordan to the east and Israel and Palestine to the west, is one of the world's saltiest bodies of water. Its high salt concentration allows swimmers to easily float on its surface.

The Great Barrier Reef, located off the coast of Queensland, Australia, is the world's largest coral reef system. It's composed of over 2,900 individual reefs and 900 islands, spanning over 1,400 miles (2,200 km).

The Caribbean Sea is home to approximately 7,000 islands. These include notable ones like Cuba, Jamaica, and Puerto Rico, and if you visited one island per day, it would take you over 19 years to see them all.

This hyper-saline sea is about ten times saltier than the typical seawater you'd find in the open ocean. The sea is also the lowest point on the Earth's surface, sitting more than 400 meters below sea level. This contributes to a unique atmospheric condition that filters out harmful UV rays, leading to a higher concentration of oxygen, making the area beneficial for health and skin treatments.

The Great Wall of China is the longest man-made structure in the world. It stretches over 13,000 miles (21,196 km), traversing various terrains and climates.

The world's largest shoe, located in Marikina, Philippines, measures over 17 feet long and 8 feet wide (5x2 m). Marikina is known as the shoe capital of the Philippines.

The Sea of Stars on Vaadhoo Island, Maldives, is a natural phenomenon that causes the shoreline to resemble a starry sky.

When tiny creatures in the water called dinoflagellates are disturbed by something like a wave, they light up in a pretty blue color. This is called bioluminescence, the same thing that makes fireflies glow. It's a neat way for these tiny organisms to try and scare off anything that might want to eat them.

Salar de Uyuni, located in Bolivia, is the world's largest salt flat. Spanning over 4,000 square miles (6,437 sq-km), it's a major breeding ground for several species of flamingos and is also a significant source of lithium.

Glass Beach, located in Fort Bragg, California, is famous for its sea glass. The glass was created from years of dumping garbage into an area of coastline near the northern part of the town.

The Grand Canyon, located in Arizona, USA, is a steep-sided canyon carved by the Colorado River. It stretches 277 miles (446 km) long and up to 18 miles (29 km) wide, making it one of the most impressive natural wonders of the world.

Son Doong Cave in Vietnam is the largest cave in the world. It extends more than 5.5 miles (8.8 km) long, with sections reaching up to 656 ft tall by 492 ft wide (200 meters tall and 150 meters wide), and offers a glimpse into an underground world that few have the opportunity to experience.

The Door to Hell is a natural gas field in Derweze, Turkmenistan. The field has been burning continuously since it was set on fire by geologists in 1971.

It was created when Soviet geologists accidentally punctured a natural gas cavern, causing it to collapse. To avoid the release of poisonous gases, they set it on fire, expecting it to burn out quickly, but it's still burning today, earning it its ominous nickname. The bright, perpetual flames have made it an unexpected tourist hotspot.

The Big Pineapple is a heritage-listed tourist attraction in Queensland, Australia. The 52 ft (16-meter) -high structure is one of Australia's best-known big things.

The Leaning Tower of Pisa in Italy is famous for its unintended tilt. The tilt began during its construction in the 12th century due to inadequate foundation on ground too soft on one side, and it has continued to increase over the centuries.

Shani Shingnapur is a village in India known for its houses with no doors, only door frames. Even the local bank operates without locks, a testament to the community's trust and faith in one another.

Mill Ends Park in Portland, Oregon, is the world's smallest park. With a diameter of just two feet (60 cm), it was originally intended to be the site for a light pole.

ANCIENT EMPIRES

This alignment is not a matter of chance; it reflects the Egyptians' detailed understanding of celestial patterns. For the ancient Egyptians, astronomy was not just a scientific endeavor, but a bridge between the earthly and divine realms. They believed their pharaohs ascended to the sky after death, joining the gods in the stars.

The term "pharaoh" translates from ancient Egyptian as "big house", initially referring to the ruler's palace, then the ruler himself. This etymology provides insight into the symbolic power of architecture in ancient Egypt.

Tombs in the pyramids were equipped with ingenious traps to protect them from looters. This reflects the importance placed on the afterlife and the measures taken to safeguard it.

Ephesus, now in Turkey, was a significant city during the Hellenistic and Roman periods. The Library of Celsus and the Temple of Artemis are among its most impressive ruins.

The Chinese civilization, dating back to around 2100 BCE, had the Shang Dynasty as its first recorded dynasty, lasting from 1600 BCE to 1046 BCE. This civilization is known for its long history and significant contributions to culture, philosophy, and technology.

Knossos, in Greece, was a major center of the Minoan Civilization. The Palace of Knossos and the Snake Goddess figurine are notable remnants of its past.

Machu Picchu, built in the 15th century, is an ancient Incan city, often referred to as the "Lost City of the Incas", located high in the Andes Mountains in Peru and a UNESCO World Heritage site.

The famous Egyptian pyramids were not built by slaves, but by skilled hired workers. This contradicts popular myths about pyramid construction.

The ancient city of Tikal, in what is now Guatemala, was a major center of Mayan civilization and was abandoned in the 10th century CE. This city is a significant archaeological site for understanding Mayan culture.

Nestled between two peaks, Machu Picchu (which means "Old Peak" in the Quechua language) is situated almost 8,000 feet (2438 m) above sea level. Its remote location and the surrounding steep mountainous terrain are likely what kept it hidden and preserved for so many centuries.

The famous Library of Alexandria, a hub for ancient inventors and philosophers, was located in Ancient Egypt. The library housed countless scrolls and texts, preserving a vast wealth of knowledge that influenced various scientific fields.

The Babylonians, an ancient civilization in Mesopotamia, existed from the 18th to the 6th century BCE. They are known for their advancements in law, literature, and science.

Petra, a mesmerizing ancient city nestled in the heart of Jordan is a true spectacle carved right out of the rosy rocks, earning it the nickname 'Rose City', Petra was founded in 312 BC and stood proud as the vibrant capital of the Nabataean Kingdom.

The city's showstopper is its iconic monument, Al-Khazneh, the "Treasury." This majestic structure, appearing to guard the city at the end of a narrow gorge, is not a treasure house as its name suggests, but rather a spectacular ceremonial tomb, displaying the impressive architectural prowess of the ancient Nabataeans.

Tulum, in Mexico, was a significant city in the Mayan Civilization. Its ruins, including the Temple of the Frescoes and the Castle, offer a glimpse into its rich history.

Cleopatra, the renowned queen of Egypt, was actually of Greek descent from Macedonia. This fact often surprises those who associate her primarily with Egypt.

The Persians, an ancient civilization in the area that is now Iran, existed from around 550 BCE to the 4th century BCE. They are known for their vast empire and contributions to art, architecture, and governance.

Chan Chan in Peru was a central city of the Chimú Civilization. The Tschudi Palace and the Huaca del Sol are among its notable ruins.

Perched atop the Acropolis, the city's highest point, the Parthenon stands as a grand symbol of Ancient Greece's artistic and architectural glory. Built in the 5th century BC, this magnificent temple was dedicated to Athena, the patron goddess of Athens.

The Mayans held a unique belief that strabismus, or crossed-eyes, was a sign of favor from their sun deity, Kinich Ahau, who was depicted with the same condition. To achieve this look, they would hang objects between their children's eyes, hoping to induce a permanent cross-eyed appearance.

The Parthenon is not just an ordinary temple. Every one of its 46 towering Doric columns showcases the ingenuity of the ancient Greeks, constructed with precision to create an optical illusion of straight lines. Struck by disaster and war over the centuries, the Parthenon has been a fortress, a church, a mosque, and even an ammunition dump!

Tiwanaku, located in present-day Bolivia, was a significant hub of the Tiwanaku Civilization. Its ruins, such as the Gate of the Sun and the Akapana Pyramid, are a testament to its past grandeur.

The ancient city of Jericho, in what is now the West Bank, is considered one of the oldest continuously inhabited cities in the world, dating back to around 8000 BCE. This city is a testament to the longevity and resilience of human settlements.

The Aztecs, an ancient civilization in Mexico, existed from the 14th to the 16th century. They are known for their complex social, political, and religious systems.

Chichen Itza, one of the most significant archaeological sites of the Mayan civilization in Mexico's Yucatan Peninsula, holds a fascinating secret. Each side of the pyramid has a stairway with 91 steps, which, added together and including the temple platform on top as the final 'step', equals the 365 days of the solar year.

The Olmecs, an ancient civilization in Mexico, existed from around 1400 BCE to 400 BCE. They are often considered the mother culture of later Mesoamerican civilizations.

Mohenjo-Daro, now in Pakistan, was a significant city of the Indus Valley Civilization. The Great Bath and the Dancing Girl figurine are among its most impressive ruins.

El Castillo, the main pyramid at Chichen Itza, is a marvel of ancient engineering and astronomical knowledge. This pyramid's design corresponds not only to the solar year but also to other celestial events. For instance, during the spring and autumn equinoxes, the setting sun casts a shadow on the pyramid creating the illusion of a serpent, Kukulcan, crawling down the steps.

In contrast to modern beauty standards, the Mayans considered a large nose to be the epitome of attractiveness. Those with smaller noses would often wear prosthetic noses made from clay to enhance their facial profile and achieve the desired look.

The ancient city of Persepolis, in what is now Iran, was the capital of the Persian Empire and was destroyed by Alexander the Great in 330 BCE. This city is a symbol of the grandeur of the ancient Persian Empire. Its glory was short-lived, as Alexander the Great laid siege to the city and destroyed it in 330 BCE.

Once the pulsating heart of the Pagan Empire, Bagan in modern-day Myanmar is now an archaeological treasure trove, boasting over 2,000 temples and pagodas that silently narrate its rich history.

The ancient Romans developed an early form of air conditioning by running cold water from aqueducts through pipes in their homes. These aqueducts also supplied water for public baths, latrines, fountains, and private households, while sewage systems efficiently disposed of wastewater into nearby water bodies.

The Aztecs held a deeply significant and rather unique view of childbirth, considering it equivalent to the fierce battles fought by warriors.

The Phoenicians, an ancient civilization in the eastern Mediterranean, existed from around 1550 BCE to 300 BCE. They are known for their seafaring skills and the creation of one of the earliest alphabets.

They believed that women who perished in childbirth ascended to the same illustrious heavens as men who fell in battle, a testament to the intensity and bravery associated with the act of bringing new life into the world. It was believed these women joined the esteemed dead who escorted the Sun from the zenith to the horizon at twilight.

Palmyra, nestled in present-day Syria, was a significant city in the ancient Palmyrene Empire, its grand ruins like the Temple of Bel and the Arch of Triumph serving as enduring testaments to its past splendor at the crossroads of Roman and Persian cultures.

The Mycenaeans, an ancient civilization in Greece, existed from around 1600 BCE to 1100 BCE. They are known for their influence on classical Greek culture and mythology.

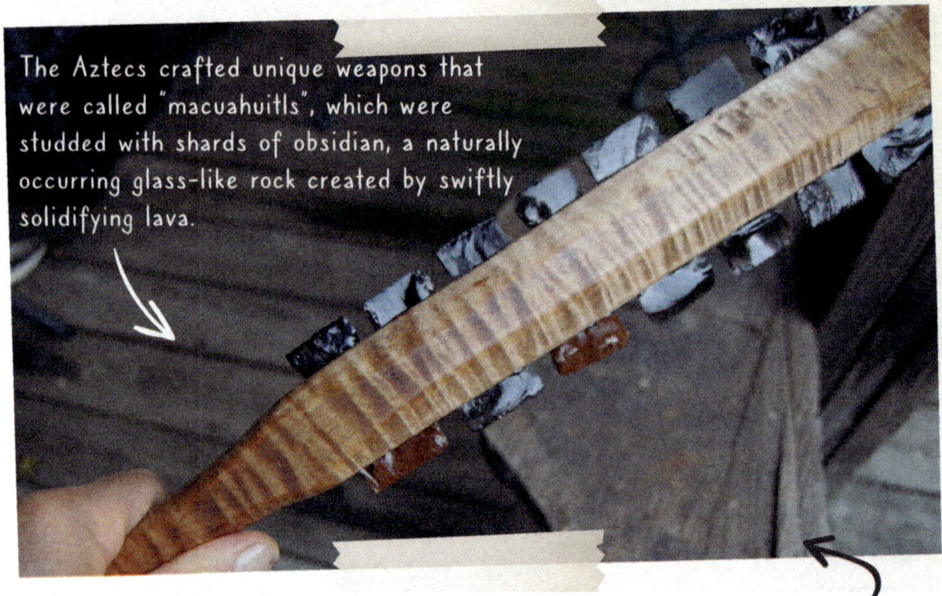

Impressively, these obsidian blades were sharper than even today's high-quality steel razor blades. Some of these deadly instruments matched the height of a full-grown man. The obsidian blades were ingeniously inlaid along the wooden core, sometimes leaving gaps between each shard, while others were set close together to form a continuous, razor-sharp edge.

The ancient city of Carthage, in what is now Tunisia, was a major power in the Mediterranean world and was eventually destroyed by the Romans in the Third Punic War. This city is a testament to the power struggles of ancient civilizations.

Egyptian Pharaoh Pepi II had a unique method of dealing with flies: he had slaves covered in honey to distract the insects. It's an intriguing anecdote that offers a glimpse into the lavish and sometimes bizarre practices of the pharaohs.

The world's first democratic government, established in ancient Greece, had a relatively short lifespan of just 185 years before succumbing to autocratic rule.

Teotihuacan, in Mexico, was a major city of the Teotihuacan Civilization. The Pyramid of the Sun and the Pyramid of the Moon are among its most impressive ruins.

The Indus Valley civilization, one of the world's oldest, thrived from around 3300 BCE to 1300 BCE. Its existence demonstrates the early development of complex societies in South Asia.

Sparta, an ancient city-state in Greece, was renowned for its disciplined, militaristic culture, and its male inhabitants, known as Spartans, lived lives deeply entrenched in military training and values. The essence of Sparta was encapsulated in its citizen-soldiers who were fiercely trained from an early age to become the embodiment of discipline, endurance, and bravery.

From as young as seven, boys underwent a rigorous state-run educational regime known as the 'agoge,' an all-encompassing institution focused on molding future warriors through physical training, survival techniques, and even subtle arts of stealth.

The ancient Greeks invented the spiked dog collar, known as a "melium," to protect sheepdogs. These collars were designed to shield the dogs' necks from wolf bites, enabling them to defend sheep flocks more effectively. The invention highlights the Greeks' practical problem-solving approach.

The Spanish Conquistadors' conquest of the Mayans led to the tragic destruction of most Mayan books. It's estimated that the Mayans had written over 10,000 books collectively, but only a handful have survived to the present day.

TECH TREASURES

Amazon was initially called Cadabra, inspired by the magical spell "abracadabra", aiming to bring a touch of magic to the growing world of online shopping.

cadabra

However, owner Jeff Bezos soon decided to change the name when a lawyer misheard Cadabra as "cadaver," not exactly the association he intended for his venture. His love for the Amazon River, the largest river in the world by volume, led him to rebrand the company as "Amazon," symbolic of the vast and diverse range of products he envisioned offering to customers across the globe.

The first spam email was sent in 1978 by Gary Thuerk to ARPANET users to sell computers. The term "spamming" was later coined in 1993 by a USENET user.

Facebook's color is blue because Mark Zuckerberg, being red-green color-blind, selected blue as it is the most visible color for him.

Myspace, once the most popular social site, lost all its data uploaded before 2016 during a server migration.

The @ symbol was used in email addresses as it was one of the least used keyboard symbols. Ray Tomlinson, when inventing email in 1971, wanted a symbol that could separate the username and host without causing confusion.

The first browser was WorldWideWeb, developed by Berners-Lee, the founder of the World Wide Web. It functioned both as a browser and as an editor.

CAPTCHA stands for "Completely Automated Public Turing test to tell Computer and Humans Apart". It is a security measure used on the web to distinguish between humans and bots.

When creating their search engine, Google's founders, Larry Page and Sergey Brin, wanted a name that could encapsulate the infinite amount of data they planned to organize. They landed on "Googol," a mathematical term representing a 1 followed by 100 zeros.

Wi-Fi isn't an acronym. Its previous name was IEEE 802.11b, which was simplified to Wi-Fi.

Google and Yahoo hired goats to mow the lawn at their headquarters to lower their carbon emissions. In 2009, Google made a contract with California Grazing to provide 200 goats to mow their Mountain View headquarters.

Queen Elizabeth II became the first royal to send an email during her visit to the Royal Signals and Radar Establishment in 1976. She sent an email using ARPANET, making her the first royal to do so.

But because of a spelling mistake made during a brainstorming meeting, "Googol" became the now-famous "Google." The founders liked this happy accident, so the name stuck. Today, Google is a symbol of how big the internet is and how the company's goal is to make information easy to find for everyone.

Berners-Lee, the inventor of the World Wide Web, regrets adding double forward slashes (after "http:") in URLs. He realized these were causing a waste of time and paper, but it was too late!

The digital world sees the creation and release of over 6,000 new computer viruses each month, a significant increase from the mere 50 known viruses in 1990.

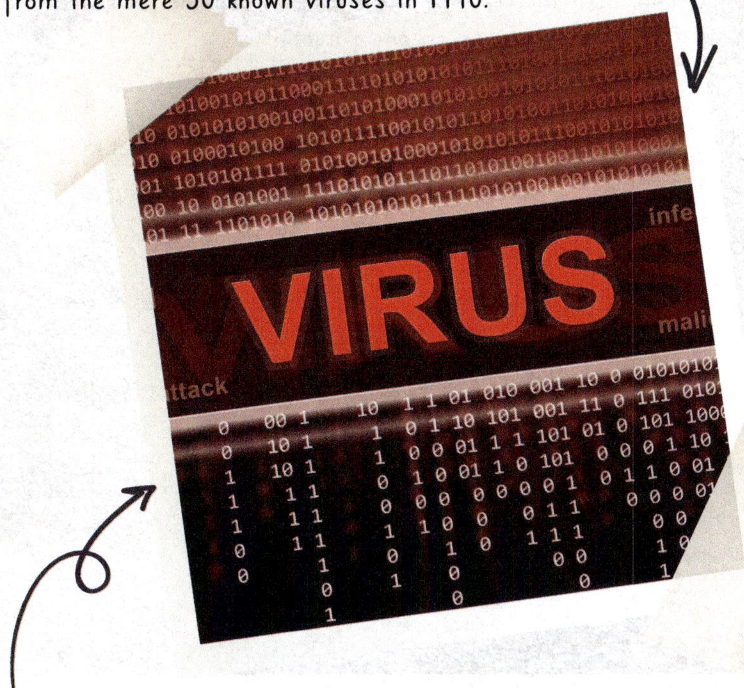

These viruses often sneak into systems through emails. It's estimated that a staggering 90% of all emails might contain a virus or malware. Many people might open an email or download an attachment without realizing they're introducing a virus to their system. This underlines the importance of having reliable and updated antivirus software to protect against these ever-evolving threats.

The first computer virus was named "Creeper" and was created in 1971 as an experiment to see how fast a message could spread from computer to computer.

The Surface Web, which is indexed by search engines, accounts for only 0.03% of the internet. The rest is the Deep Web, which is 400 times larger.

Reading on a screen slows down your reading speed by 10% compared to reading physical pages.

The original Xbox featured snippets from real transmissions from the Apollo space missions.

Approximately 86% of people try to insert their USBs upside down on the first attempt.

According to former Air Force launch officer Bruce Blair, the password for nuclear missiles was simply '00000000' for 20 years. Despite the Air Force's denial, Blair insists this was the case, and the password was even written down to ensure no one forgot it.

iTunes' terms and conditions state that users are not to use their devices to create nuclear, missile, or chemical or biological weapons.

The phenomenon of thinking your phone is vibrating when it's not is called Phantom Vibration Syndrome.

Amazon's Alexa is always listening to improve your user experience by storing your conversations in the cloud.

Even though the U.S. Air Force denied these claims, Mr. Blair stands by what he said. Could you imagine knowing that something as destructive as a nuclear missile had a password as easy as '00000000'? It's important to remember that these days, security around such serious things has likely gotten a lot stronger!

Nintendo, originally founded in 1889 as a playing card company, made its debut in the video game industry with the Color TV-Game series in 1977. This marked the beginning of Nintendo's transformation into a globally recognized video game powerhouse.

Surgeons who played video games for more than three hours a week during their childhood make 37% fewer errors and perform laparoscopic surgery 42% faster.

All Apple iPhone ads show the time as 9:41 a.m., which is the exact time that Steve Jobs announced the first iPhone in 2007.

Believe it or not, there are technology-related phobias, including Technophobia (fear of technology), Cyberphobia (fear of computers), and Nomophobia (fear of being without your phone).

More people in the world have mobile phones than toilets, with over 6 billion people having mobile phones compared to 4.5 billion people having working toilets.

A Nintendo Game Boy was taken to space by cosmonaut Aleksandr Serebrov during the Soyuz TM-17 space mission in 1993.

In our rapidly evolving digital world, it's no surprise that new phobias, or irrational fears, have emerged related to technology. The idea of using new gadgets, understanding complex machines, or even just keeping up with the pace of technological advancements can induce a significant amount of stress in individuals with this fear. It's a fascinating insight into how our brains are adapting (or sometimes struggling to adapt) to the rapid progression of technology in our lives!

The QWERTY keyboard layout was designed to slow typists down to prevent key jams on early typewriters. By placing frequently used letters apart, it reduced mechanical collisions, and the design continues to be used today.

Wikipedia, with its 54 million pages, relies on an army of 2,456 automated bots to keep its vast repository of knowledge well-maintained and up-to-date.

The record for the most expensive phone number was set in 2006 during a charity auction hosted by Qatar Telecom. The number 666-6666 was sold to an anonymous bidder for a staggering $2.75 million.

In 2010, The United States government used PlayStation 3's, but not for gaming!

The digital age has revolutionized the way American couples meet, with 40% of couples who got together in 2017 having met online. Interestingly, the traditional method of meeting through friends saw a 13% decline from 1995 to 2017.

The U.S. Air Force found a clever way to build a supercomputer without spending a ton of money or using a lot of energy. They used 1,760 PlayStation 3 consoles, which were already powerful and didn't use much energy. This "green" supercomputer could do complex tasks like improving radar and processing satellite images. So, the PlayStation 3 consoles were not just for gaming, they also helped with national defense!

The term "Silver Surfers" has been coined to describe the relatively rare group of seniors over 50 who regularly use the internet. Despite the digital age, this demographic remains a minority among internet users.

Google processes approximately 99,000 search queries every second, totaling to 8.5 billion searches every day.

Imagine looking up at the night sky and knowing that the twinkling lights aren't just stars, but also satellites providing internet to people around the world. This isn't a scene from a sci-fi movie, but the reality of SpaceX's Starlink project.

Imagine a world where high-speed internet is accessible from every corner of the globe, even the most remote locations. Utilizing a constellation of satellites orbiting closer to Earth than traditional ones, Starlink aims to provide faster, smoother internet service with less lag, even in places that don't have access to the internet. So, as you gaze up at the night sky, remember that among the stars, there might be a Starlink satellite, part of a project that's revolutionizing our internet and our view of what's possible.

There are fake Apple Stores in China that sometimes sell legitimate Apple products but often use counterfeit parts for repairs.

We delete 90% of the apps we download due to various reasons such as usability issues, sneaky subscriptions, or lack of space on our phones.

Apple ventured into the clothing business after Steve Jobs left the company in 1985. Launching "The Apple Collection" in 1986, the move surprised many and marked a departure from their tech roots. Unfortunately, the clothing line failed miserably and is now a little-known chapter in the company's history.

The amount of power required to fuel Google's vast range of services, from search and email to cloud storage and machine learning, is breathtaking. In 2020 alone, Google consumed 15.5 terawatt-hours of energy. To put that into perspective, this is twice the amount of power used by the entire city of San Francisco.

The reason behind Google's colossal power consumption lies in the intensive energy demands of data centers. Data centers house thousands of servers, which process and store information for billions of users. These servers need to be powered up and cooled constantly, which results in a large energy footprint. In addition, energy is also consumed in maintaining the vast physical infrastructure, security systems, lighting, and the cooling necessary to keep these data centers from overheating.

In total, only 21 million Bitcoins will ever be mined. The purpose of this cap is to generate artificial scarcity, much like gold. A long-term and fascinating phenomenon in the world of finance, Bitcoin's mining process slows down with time due to built-in complexity, and the last Bitcoin is not projected to be mined until around the distant year 2140.

The GPS system, initially invented by the U.S. military, is now used by the entire world for free. However, it costs almost 2 million dollars per day to operate.

The three most popular passwords also happen to be the weakest. "123456," "password," and "12345" are all in the list.

Dear reader,

First and foremost, I want to express my heartfelt gratitude for choosing my book to share with your family. I sincerely hope that you have found joy, learning, and inspiration within these pages.

As an author, I pour my heart and soul into creating books that not only entertain but also provide valuable experiences. Your feedback is incredibly important to me and helps me to continue creating content that resonates with readers around the world.

If you enjoyed reading this book I kindly ask you to consider leaving a review.

I want you to know that I will personally read each and every review. Your thoughts mean a great deal to me. To make this process as seamless as possible, I have included a QR code here that you can scan, which will directly take you to the Amazon review page.

Thank you for your support and for giving my book a chance to spark imagination, wonder, and learning in your family's lives.

Happy reading,

Riley Wolfe

Printed in Great Britain
by Amazon